The Hebridean Pocket Diary 2014

Illustrations by Mairi Hedderwick

This edition first published in 2013 by
Birlinn Limited
West Newington House
10 Newington Road
Edinburgh
EH9 1QS

www.birlinn.co.uk

ISBN: 978 1 78027 125 5

British Library Cataloguing-in-Publication Data
A Catalogue record for this book is available from the British Library

Printed and bound in China

These Hebridean sketches have been garnered over a period of forty years – some whilst living on one of the islands, others as I escaped from mainland exile. Some landmarks are no more – a post box disappeared, the old pier superseded by the new, many hens long gone into the pot. The mountains and headlands and the horizon line of the sea, however, never change – or diminish. And neither do the midges.

The Clyde islands are not truly Hebridean, but as one set of my forebears hailed from Corrie, on Arran, I am sure they will be pleased at their inclusion, as I hope you are with this Hebridean diary.

Mairi Hedderwick

2014

January Am Faoilleach

M	T	W	T	F	S	S
		1	2	3	4	5
6	7	8	9	10	11	12
13	14	15	16	17	18	19
20	21	22	23	24	25	26
27	28	29	30	31		

February An Gearran

M	T	W	T	F	S	S
					1	2
3	4	5	6	7	8	9
10	11	12	13	14	15	16
17	18	19	20	21	22	23
24	25	26	27	28		

March Am Màrt

M	T	W	T	F	S	S
					1	2
3	4	5	6	7	8	9
10	11	12	13	14	15	16
17	18	19	20	21	22	23
24	25	26	27	28	29	30
31						

April An Giblean

M	T	W	T	F	S	S
	1	2	3	4	5	6
7	8	9	10	11	12	13
14	15	16	17	18	19	20
21	22	23	24	25	26	27
28	29	30				

May An Cèitean

M	T	W	T	F	S	S
			1	2	3	4
5	6	7	8	9	10	11
12	13	14	15	16	17	18
19	20	21	22	23	24	25
26	27	28	29	30	31	

June An t-Ògmhios

M	T	W	T	F	S	S
						1
2	3	4	5	6	7	8
9	10	11	12	13	14	15
16	17	18	19	20	21	22
23	24	25	26	27	28	29
30						

July An t-Iuchar

M	T	W	T	F	S	S
	1	2	3	4	5	6
7	8	9	10	11	12	13
14	15	16	17	18	19	20
21	22	23	24	25	26	27
28	29	30	31			

August An Lùnastal

M	T	W	T	F	S	S
				1	2	3
4	5	6	7	8	9	10
11	12	13	14	15	16	17
18	19	20	21	22	23	24
25	26	27	28	29	30	31

September An t-Sultain

M	T	W	T	F	S	S
1	2	3	4	5	6	7
8	9	10	11	12	13	14
15	16	17	18	19	20	21
22	23	24	25	26	27	28
29	30					

October An Dàmhair

M	T	W	T	F	S	S
		1	2	3	4	5
6	7	8	9	10	11	12
13	14	15	16	17	18	19
20	21	22	23	24	25	26
27	28	29	30	31		

November An t-Samhain

M	T	W	T	F	S	S
					1	2
3	4	5	6	7	8	9
10	11	12	13	14	15	16
17	18	19	20	21	22	23
24	25	26	27	28	29	30

December An Dùbhlachd

M	T	W	T	F	S	S
1	2	3	4	5	6	7
8	9	10	11	12	13	14
15	16	17	18	19	20	21
22	23	24	25	26	27	28
29	30	31				

2015

January Am Faoilleach

M	T	W	T	F	S	S
			1	2	3	4
5	6	7	8	9	10	11
12	13	14	15	16	17	18
19	20	21	22	23	24	25
26	27	28	29	30	31	

February An Gearran

M	T	W	T	F	S	S
						1
2	3	4	5	6	7	8
9	10	11	12	13	14	15
16	17	18	19	20	21	22
23	24	25	26	27	28	

March Am Màrt

M	T	W	T	F	S	S
						1
2	3	4	5	6	7	8
9	10	11	12	13	14	15
16	17	18	19	20	21	22
23	24	25	26	27	28	29
30	31					

April An Giblean

M	T	W	T	F	S	S
		1	2	3	4	5
6	7	8	9	10	11	12
13	14	15	16	17	18	19
20	21	22	23	24	25	26
27	28	29	30			

May An Cèitean

M	T	W	T	F	S	S
				1	2	3
4	5	6	7	8	9	10
11	12	13	14	15	16	17
18	19	20	21	22	23	24
25	26	27	28	29	30	31

June An t-Ògmhios

M	T	W	T	F	S	S
1	2	3	4	5	6	7
8	9	10	11	12	13	14
15	16	17	18	19	20	21
22	23	24	25	26	27	28
29	30					

July An t-Iuchar

M	T	W	T	F	S	S
		1	2	3	4	5
6	7	8	9	10	11	12
13	14	15	16	17	18	19
20	21	22	23	24	25	26
27	28	29	30	31		

August An Lùnastal

M	T	W	T	F	S	S
					1	2
3	4	5	6	7	8	9
10	11	12	13	14	15	16
17	18	19	20	21	22	23
24	25	26	27	28	29	30
31						

September An t-Sultain

M	T	W	T	F	S	S
	1	2	3	4	5	6
7	8	9	10	11	12	13
14	15	16	17	18	19	20
21	22	23	24	25	26	27
28	29	30				

October An Dàmhair

M	T	W	T	F	S	S
			1	2	3	4
5	6	7	8	9	10	11
12	13	14	15	16	17	18
19	20	21	22	23	24	25
26	27	28	29	30	31	

November An t-Samhain

M	T	W	T	F	S	S
						1
2	3	4	5	6	7	8
9	10	11	12	13	14	15
16	17	18	19	20	21	22
23	24	25	26	27	28	29
30						

December An Dùbhlachd

M	T	W	T	F	S	S
	1	2	3	4	5	6
7	8	9	10	11	12	13
14	15	16	17	18	19	20
21	22	23	24	25	26	27
28	29	30	31			

The Butt of Lewis.

Monday Diluain   16

Tuesday Dimàirt   17

Wednesday Diciadain   18

Thursday Diardaoin   19

Friday Dihaoine   20

Saturday Disathairne   Winter Solstice   21
                                Grian-stad a' Gheamhraidh

Sunday Didòmhnaich   22

December
An Dùbhlachd

---

23   **Monday** Diluain

---

24   Christmas Eve
      Oidhche nam Bannag   **Tuesday** Dimàirt

---

25   Christmas Day
      Là na Nollaige   **Wednesday** Diciadain

---

26   Boxing Day Là nam Bogsa   **Thursday** Diardaoin

Friday Dihaoine

27

Saturday Disathairne

28

Sunday Didòmhnaich

29

Cairns of Coll · Rum beyond

December January 2014

An Dùbhlachd / Am Faoilleach

30		Monday Diluain
31	Hogmanay Oidhche Challainn	Tuesday Dimàirt
1	New Year's Day Là na Bliadhn' Ùire	Wednesday Diciadain
2	Bank Holiday (Scotland) Là-fèill Banca	Thursday Diardaoin
3		Friday Dihaoine
4		Saturday Disathairne
5		Sunday Didòmhnaich

— Winter
Main St. Coll.   La Sitooterie ~

January
Am Faoilleach

6   **Monday** Diluain

7   **Tuesday** Dimàirt

8   **Wednesday** Diciadain

9   **Thursday** Diardaoin

Shearwater returning from Muck

Friday Dihaoine | **10**

Saturday Disathairne | **11**

Sunday Didòmhnaich | Old New Year
An t-Seann Bhliadhn' Ùr | **12**

· The Mainland from the Sgurr of Eigg ·

January
Am Faoilleach

13   Monday Diluain

14   Tuesday Dimàirt

15   Wednesday Diciadain

16   Thursday Diardaoin

Oystercatcher.

Friday Dihaoine

17

Saturday Disathairne

18

Sunday Didòmhnaich

19

Port à' Raidhlein .
Portnahaven . Islay.

January
Am Faoilleach

| 20 | **Monday** Diluain |

| 21 | **Tuesday** Dimàirt |

| 22 | **Wednesday** Diciadain |

| 23 | **Thursday** Diardaoin |

· Callanish Stones ·
Lewis

Friday Dihaoine   24

Saturday Disathairne   **Burns Night** Fèill Burns   25

Sunday Didòmhnaich   26

27	**Monday** Diluain

28	**Tuesday** Dimàirt

29	**Wednesday** Diciadain

30	**Thursday** Diardaoin

· Harris · Loch Seaforth Border · Lewis ·

— Bowmore Distillery
· ISLAY · —Furnace—

Friday Dihaoine

31

Saturday Disathairne   St Bride's Day Là Fhèill Brighde

1

Sunday Didòmhnaich   Candlemas
                            Là Fhèill Moire nan Coinnlean

2

February

An Gearran

3   Monday Diluain

4   Tuesday Dimàirt

5   Wednesday Diciadain

Thursday Diardaoin

6

Friday Dihaoine

7

Saturday Disathairne

8

Sunday Didòmhnaich

9

Garrynahine

Isle of Lewis

February
An Gearran

---

10   Monday Diluain

---

11   Tuesday Dimàirt

---

12   Wednesday Diciadain

---

13   Thursday Diardaoin

From Orbost looking out to Harlosh. Skye.

Friday Dihaoine	St Valentine's Day Là Fhèill Uailein	**14**
Saturday Disathairne		**15**
Sunday Didòmhnaich		**16**

LEWIS

Port of Ness

Boats pulled
up for the
winter

February
An Gearran

Monday Diluain   17

Tuesday Dimàirt   18

Wednesday Diciadain   19

Thursday Diardaoin   20

Friday Dihaoine   21

Saturday Disathairne   22

Sunday Didòmhnaich   23

February

An Gearran

24   **Monday** Diluain

25   **Tuesday** Dimàirt

26   **Wednesday** Diciadain

Salum

Scarinish

TIREE HOUSES
Thatched Black Felters,
Pudding & Plain.

Bishop's Isles from Sea Cuter · Bhatasaidh ·

February March
An Gearran / Am Màrt

Thursday Diardaoin	27

Friday Dihaoine	28

Saturday Disathairne	St David's Day Là Fhèill Dhaibhidh	1

Sunday Didòmhnaich	2

Am Màrt

3   **Monday** Diluain

4   Shrove Tuesday Dimàirt Inid   **Tuesday** Dimàirt

5   Ash Wednesday Diciadain na Luaithre   **Wednesday** Diciadain

6   **Thursday** Diardaoin

7   **Friday** Dihaoine

8   **Saturday** Disathairne

9   **Sunday** Didòmhnaich

Stornoway Castle
hardly visible

Seagulls peevishly bemoaning the
Sabbath Still

· LEWIS ·

Y6

CRAIGNAIR

Crossapol House
& the Graveyard falling
into the sea
. coll .

March

Am Màrt

---

10   Monday Diluain

---

11   Tuesday Dimàirt

---

12   Wednesday Diciadain

---

13   Thursday Diardaoin

Friday Dihaoine 14

Saturday Disathairne 15

Sunday Didòmhnaich 16

URAGAIG
COLONSAY

Old Pier · Salen
MULL

March

Am Màrt

17 St Patrick's Day
Là Fhèill Pàdraig

Monday Diluain

18

Tuesday Dimàirt

19

Wednesday Diciadain

Thursday Diardaoin	Vernal Equinox Co-fhad-thràth an Earraich	20
Friday Dihaoine		21
Saturday Disathairne		22
Sunday Didòmhnaich		23

March

Am Màrt

24
Monday Diluain

25
Tuesday Dimàirt

26
Wednesday Diciadain

27
Thursday Diardaoin

Friday Dihaoine 28

Saturday Disathairne 29

Sunday Didòmhnaich 30

British Summer Time begins
Uair Shamhraidh Bhreatainn

Mothers' Day
Là nam Màthair

'Rossie' Burn.

Glen Rosa mountains.
from Brodick Bay
ARRAN

31
Monday Diluain

1
April Fools' Day Là na Gogaireachd
Tuesday Dimàirt

2
Wednesday Diciadain

3
Thursday Diardaoin

4
Friday Dihaoine

50 yrs. service.
Mr. Henderson raking over the vegetable garden for the last time.
Achamore Gardens. GIGHA.

MUCK
Telephone
Box

The Storm Came
Tues. Day of
supposed departure

LOCH EARBOL
TIREE

April
An Giblean

Monday Diluain 7

Tuesday Dimàirt 8

Wednesday Diciadain 9

Thursday Diardaoin 10

Friday Dihaoine 11

Saturday Disathairne 12

Sunday Didòmhnaich   **Palm Sunday** Didòmhnaich Tùrnais 13

April

An Giblean

14

15
Tuesday Dimàirt

16
Wednesday Diciadain

17 Maundy Thursday
Diardaoin a' Bhrochain Mhòir

Thursday Diardaoin

POTTIE no ① MULL

Elspeth, Lin o Prince o the last feed of the day. Burg behind

Easter Sunday. Holy Isle, Arran from St Blane's, Bute
(long after the dawn has risen.)

Friday Dihaoine   Good Friday Dihaoine na Càisge   **18**

Saturday Disathairne   **19**

Sunday Didòmhnaich   Easter Sunday **20**
Didòmhnaich na Càisge

April

An Giblean

---

21   Easter Monday Diluain na Càisge   Monday Diluain

---

22   Tuesday Dimàirt

---

23   St George's Day   Wednesday Diciadain
        Là an Naoimh Seòras

---

24   Thursday Diardaoin

---

25   Friday Dihaoine

---

26   Saturday Disathairne

---

27   Sunday Didòmhnaich

Everyone enviously watching
the rubber dinghy from the yacht
making for landfall on Staffa
after our abortive attempt.

The helicopter or the flying cement mixer

Fingal's Cave

28

29

30

1
May Day or Beltane
Là Buidhe Bealltainn

Sunday silence

No wind · Oily slap of slow waves

Balemartine
TIREE

peevish chirping of sparrows

v. puny late lamb — tethered.

YOU'LL WARM TO

COAL

FROM YOUR

Entrance Porch
WEST HIGHLAND CROFTERS & FARMERS LTd.
Lochboisdale
S. UIST

| Monday Diluain | Bank Holiday Là-fèill Banca | 5 |

| Tuesday Dimàirt | | 6 |

| Wednesday Diciadain | | 7 |

| Thursday Diardaoin | | 8 |

| Friday Dihaoine | | 9 |

| Saturday Disathairne | | 10 |

| Sunday Didòmhnaich | | 11 |

May

An Cèitean

---

12 — Monday Diluain

---

13 — Tuesday Dimàirt

---

14 — Wednesday Diciadain

---

15 — Thursday Diardaoin

---

16 — Friday Dihaoine

Colonsay

· The Heronry · Gallanach · Coll ·

Saturday Disathairne

17

Sunday Didòmhnaich

18

May

An Cèitean

19	Monday Diluain

20	Tuesday Dimàirt

21	Wednesday Diciadain

22	Thursday Diardaoin

23	Friday Dihaoine

24	Saturday Disathairne

25	Sunday Didòmhnaich

IMPORTANT NOTICE
TO VISITORS
TO THE WESTERN ISLES

ROAD SIGNS IN THE WESTERN ISLES

As part of it's policy in preserving the Gaelic
language, the Western Isles Council has adopted
a policy of Gaelic place names throughout the
Western Isles, except in the anglicized areas
of Stornoway and Benbecula where the
names are in both Gaelic and English

The Ramp jammed
Castlebay Arrive 9.00pm
Perishables hand off. loaded
We go on to S. Uist
at 10.30 pm.

BARRA

AL-MAC
17

Lochranza · Arran ·

May
An Cèitean

26	Spring Bank Holiday Là-fèill Banca an Earraich	Monday Diluain
27		Tuesday Dimàirt
28		Wednesday Diciadain
29	Ascension Day Deasghabhail	Thursday Diardaoin

May June
An Cèitean / An t-Ògmhios

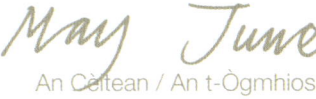

Friday Dihaoine 30

Saturday Disathairne 31

Sunday Didòmhnaich 1

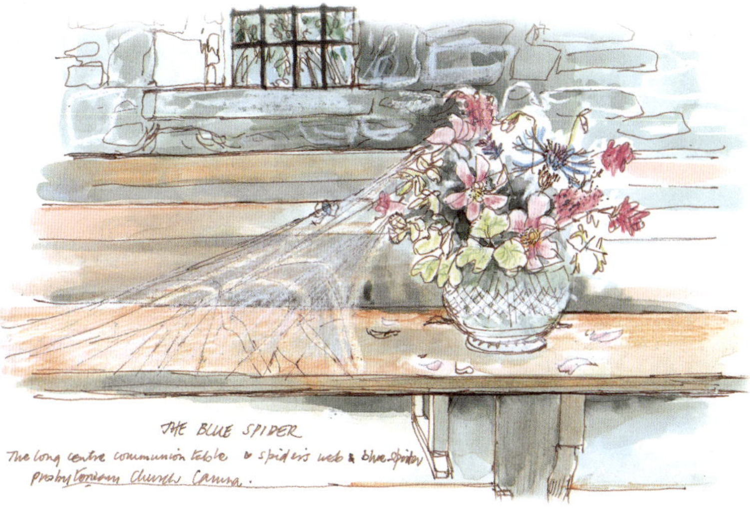

THE BLUE SPIDER
The long centre communion table & spider's web & blue spider
Presbyterian Church Canna.

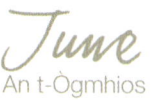

June
An t-Ògmhios

2 Monday Diluain

3 Tuesday Dimàirt

4 Wednesday Diciadain

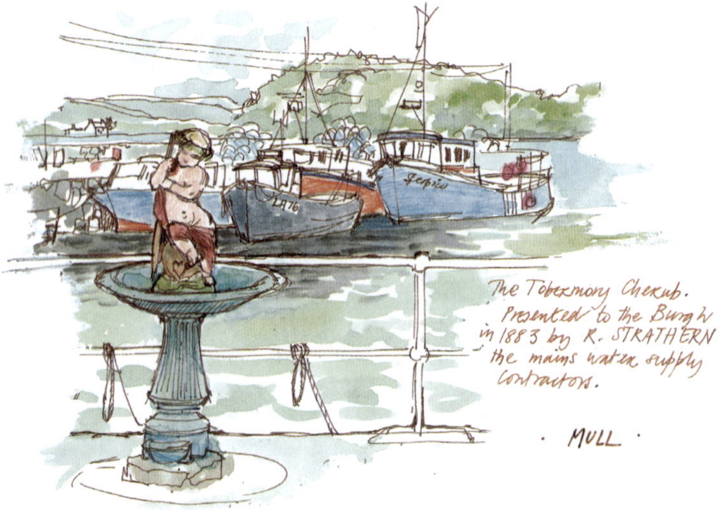

LA76
The Tobermory Cherub.
Presented to the Burgh
in 1883 by R. STRATHERN
the mains water supply
contractors.
· MULL ·

The Heatwave · Traigh Eais.

Thursday Diardaoin   5

Friday Dihaoine   6

Saturday Disathairne   7

Sunday Didòmhnaich   Whit Sunday or Pentecost   8
                                Didòmhnaich na Caingis

SCADABAY

· HARRIS ·

Mrs. Martin's
doorway
with dyed sheep's
wool & a ginger cat.

June

An t-Ògmhios

| Monday Diluain | St Columba's Day | 9 |
| | Là Fhèill Chaluim Chille | |

Tuesday Dimàirt 10

Wednesday Diciadain 11

Thursday Diardaoin 12

Friday Dihaoine 13

Saturday Disathairne 14

Sunday Didòmhnaich   Fathers' Day Là nan Athair 15

June
An t-Ògmhios

16	**Monday** Diluain
17	**Tuesday** Dimàirt
18	**Wednesday** Diciadain
19	**Thursday** Diardaoin

Friday Dihaoine 20

Saturday Disathairne Summer Solstice 21
Grian-stad an t-Samhraidh

Sunday Didòmhnaich 22

Leaving Canna
cuillens behind

June

An t-Ògmhios

| 23 | Monday Diluain |

| 24 | Tuesday Dimàirt |

| 25 | Wednesday Diciadain |

| 26 | Thursday Diardaoin |

| 27 | Friday Dihaoine |

| 28 | Saturday Disathairne |

| 29 | Sunday Didòmhnaich |

Gometra House & the
Dangerous Stags.

June July

An t-Ògmhios / An t-Iuchar

30	Monday Diluain

1	Tuesday Dimàirt

2	Wednesday Diciadain

3	Thursday Diardaoin

Glen

Friday Dihaoine 4

Saturday Disathairne 5

Sunday Didòmhnaich 6

Goatfell

Corriegills
Isle of Arran

July
An t-Iuchar

The Clown Jewels
Resting at Eoligarry Barra.

7	Monday Diluain

8	Tuesday Dimàirt

9	Wednesday Diciadain

10	Thursday Diardaoin

CASTLEBAY
A Sunday Afternoon
& then the coal boat
came in ....
BARRA

July
An t-Iuchar

14   Monday Diluain

15   St Swithun's Day   Tuesday Dimàirt
      Là Fhèill Màrtainn Builg

16   Wednesday Diciadain

17   Thursday Diardaoin

18   Friday Dihaoine

· Ruth's back door ·

· COLL ·

Tobhar na Camachachd
Well of the Journey.

Well near Cullipool
Luing.

cushions of Marsh Saxifrage
stellar clumps of primroses.

"There was not a horse that would ever go by
that well once it had had a drink from it.
The horses with the milk carts! Ach, you just had
to wait & let them have their fill." Reminisced
Irene McLachlan.

July 22
Kildonnan Eigg.

Already the purple bloom of flowering
bell heather!

Monday Diluain 21

Tuesday Dimàirt 22

Wednesday Diciadain 23

Thursday Diardaoin 24

Friday Dihaoine 25

Saturday Disathairne 26

Sunday Didòmhnaich 27

July

An t-Iuchar

28	Monday Diluain
29	Tuesday Dimàirt
30	Wednesday Diciadain
31	Thursday Diardaoin

· Tobermory · Mull ·

MONDAY is the best day to move house
from North to South.

St. Kilda · Fulmars

August

An Lùnastal

Friday Dihaoine   1

Saturday Disathairne   2

Sunday Didòmhnaich   3

August

An Lùnastal

---

4 Summer Bank Holiday (Scotland)   **Monday** Diluain
    Là-fèill Banca an t-Samhraidh

---

5   **Tuesday** Dimàirt

---

6   **Wednesday** Diciadain

Kumquats & Grapes
- Waternish Skye

Lochranza Garden
· ARRAN ·

Thursday Diardaoin
7

Friday Dihaoine
8

Saturday Disathairne
9

Sunday Didòmhnaich
10

August

An Lùnastal

11
Monday Diluain

12
Tuesday Dimàirt

End of the metalled rd.
N. Fearns ?
Raasay

The Stone of Tarbert
The Druid Stone Gigha

Wednesday Diciadain   13

Thursday Diardaoin   14

Friday Dihaoine   15

Saturday Disathairne   16

Sunday Didòmhnaich   17

August

An Lùnastal

18	Monday Diluain

19	Tuesday Dimàirt

20	Wednesday Diciadain

21	Thursday Diardaoin

Friday Dihaoine

22

Saturday Disathairne

23

Sunday Didòmhnaich

24

·Grass Point · Lochdon · MULL

August

An Lùnastal

---

25 Summer Bank Holiday (Scotland)
Là-fèill Banca an t-Samhraidh

Monday Diluain

26

Tuesday Dimàirt

27

Wednesday Diciadain

28

Thursday Diardaoin

Tiree — the blues &
turquoises
almost obscene.

Early Morning .
Tiree Window .

Friday Dihaoine

29

Saturday Disathairne

30

Sunday Didòmhnaich

31

Bell from S.M.S. DERPFLINGER

Eriskay

September
An t-Sultain

Monday Diluain 1

Tuesday Dimàirt 2

Wednesday Diciadain 3

Thursday Diardaoin 4

Friday Dihaoine 5

Saturday Disathairne 6

Sunday Didòmhnaich 7

The 'Gas Guzzler' heads on — westwards
Oban Bay   1·00 pm

September
An t-Sultain

8	Monday Diluain

9	Tuesday Dimàirt

10	Wednesday Diciadain

"Follow 'im — he seems to know the way…"

Thursday Diardaoin 11

Friday Dihaoine 12

Saturday Disathairne 13

Sunday Didòmhnaich 14

September

An t-Sultain

| 15 | Monday Diluain |

| 16 | Tuesday Dimàirt |

| 17 | Wednesday Diciadain |

| 18 | Thursday Diardaoin |

| 19 | Friday Dihaoine |

| 20 | Saturday Disathairne |

| 21 | Sunday Didòmhnaich |

SKYE

ELLISHADER

Dugald Ross's
Museum

Nearly all items one man's collection.
A lot of the bottles came from Loch
Mealt where prehistoric CHAR fish
kill off any other introductions.

September

An t-Sultain

| 22 | | Monday Diluain |

| 23 | Autumnal Equinox
Co-fhad-thràth an Fhoghair | Tuesday Dimàirt |

| 24 | | Wednesday Diciadain |

| 25 | | Thursday Diardaoin |

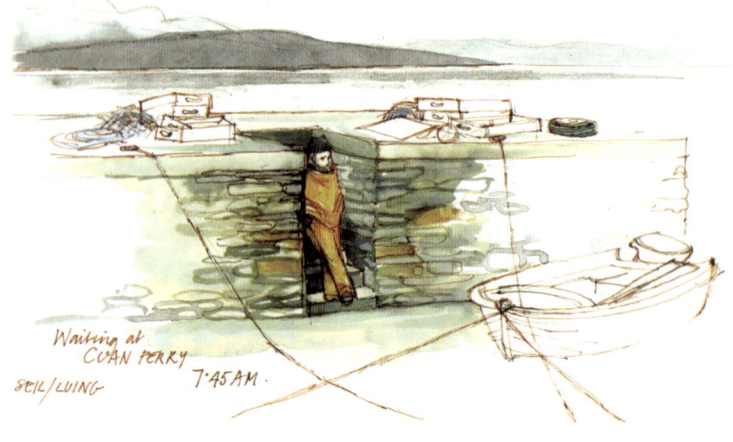

Waiting at
CUAN FERRY   7.45 AM.
SEIL/LUING

Neist Skye

Friday Dihaoine 26

Saturday Disathairne 27

Sunday Didòmhnaich 28

September October

An t-Sultain / An Dàmhair

| 29 | Michaelmas Là Fhèill Mìcheil | Monday Diluain |

| 30 | | Tuesday Dimàirt |

| 1 | | Wednesday Diciadain |

| 2 | | Thursday Diardaoin |

Shags
Muck

Port Mor
Muck

Friday Dihaoine

3

Saturday Disathairne

4

Sunday Didòmhnaich

Grandparents' Day
Latha nan Seanmhair 's nan Seanair

5

October
An Dàmhair

6

7
Tuesday Dimàirt

Taigh Chearsabhagh & The Shell Fish · N. Uist

Wednesday Diciadain   8

Thursday Diardaoin   9

Friday Dihaoine   10

Saturday Disathairne   11

Sunday Didòmhnaich   12

· Wren ·
· St.Kilda ·

October

An Dàmhair

| 13 | Monday Diluain |

| 14 | Tuesday Dimàirt |

| 15 | Wednesday Diciadain |

| 16 | Thursday Diardaoin |

| 17 | Friday Dihaoine |

| 18 | Saturday Disathairne |

| 19 | Sunday Didòmhnaich |

St. Kilda.   March Past.

Na Cuir Luath Theth Ann
(No Hot Ashes)
Deserted House
north of LOCHMADDY

N. UIST

October
An Dàmhair

Monday Diluain — 20

Tuesday Dimàirt — 21

Wednesday Diciadain — 22

Thursday Diardaoin — 23

Friday Dihaoine — 24

Saturday Disathairne — 25

Sunday Didòmhnaich — 26

British Summer Time ends
Crìoch Uair Shamhraidh Bhreatainn

October   November

An Dàmhair / An t-Samhain

| 27 | | Monday Diluain |

| 28 | | Tuesday Dimàirt |

| 29 | | Wednesday Diciadain |

| 30 | | Thursday Diardaoin |

| 31 | Hallowe'en Oidhche Shamhna | Friday Dihaoine |

| 1 | All Saints' Day Fèill nan Uile Naomh | Saturday Disathairne |

| 2 | | Sunday Didòmhnaich |

Bowmore · Isle of Islay.

November

An t-Samhain

3	**Monday** Diluain

4	**Tuesday** Dimàirt

5	Guy Fawkes' Night Oidhche Ghuy Fawkes	**Wednesday** Diciadain

6	**Thursday** Diardaoin

Holy Isle ARRAN

The Cottage
Stormy Hill
PORTREE

· SKYE ·

Friday Dihaoine   7

Saturday Disathairne   8

Sunday Didòmhnaich   Remembrance Sunday   9
                                        Didòmhnaich Cuimhneachaidh

November

An t-Samhain

| 10 | Monday Diluain |

| 11 | Martinmas Là Fhèill Màrtainn | Tuesday Dimàirt |

| 12 | Wednesday Diciadain |

| 13 | Thursday Diardaoin |

| 14 | Friday Dihaoine |

Tikeo

Castlebay
BARRA
from
Heaval

Saturday Disathairne

15

Sunday Didòmhnaich

16

Ardtalla · ISLAY...15

Recyled
cattle troughs.

Monday Diluain	17
Tuesday Dimàirt	18
Wednesday Diciadain	19
Thursday Diardaoin	20
Friday Dihaoine	21
Saturday Disathairne	22
Sunday Didòmhnaich	23

November

An t-Samhain

24	Monday Diluain

25	Tuesday Dimàirt

26	Wednesday Diciadain

27	Thursday Diardaoin

Screeching Tern

- Benbecula.
- The old incorporated
into the new.

Friday Dihaoine

28

Saturday Disathairne

29

Sunday Didòmhnaich

St Andrew's Day
Là an Naoimh Anndras

30

December
An Dùbhlachd

1   **Monday** Diluain

2   **Tuesday** Dimàirt

3   **Wednesday** Diciadain

4   **Thursday** Diardaoin

The Storr
. Isle of Skye .

Friday Dihaoine

5

Saturday Disathairne

6

Sunday Didòmhnaich

7

Gylen
Castle.
Kerrera.

'Lord of the Isles'
— Leaving Oban

December
An Dùbhlachd

8	Monday Diluain

9	Tuesday Dimàirt

10	Wednesday Diciadain

11	Thursday Diardaoin

MULL BEYOND

Friday Dihaoine   12

Saturday Disathairne   13

Sunday Didòmhnaich   14

December
An Dùbhlachd

15
Monday Diluain

16
Tuesday Dimàirt

17
Wednesday Diciadain

The Black Box — The Phone Box   Eigg.

Jura · Evening · Above Corran Sands

Thursday Diardaoin	18

Friday Dihaoine	19

Saturday Disathairne	20

Sunday Didòmhnaich	Winter Solstice Grian-stad a' Gheamhraidh	21

Shrine
IOCHDAR.
S. UIST.

Monday Diluain 22

Tuesday Dimàirt 23

Wednesday Diciadain | Christmas Eve
Oidhche nam Bannag | 24

Thursday Diardaoin | Christmas Day
Là na Nollaige | 25

Friday Dihaoine | Boxing Day
Là nam Bogsa | 26

Saturday Disathairne 27

Sunday Didòmhnaich 28

December January 2015

An Dùbhlachd / Am Faoilleach

29 — Monday Diluain

30 — Tuesday Dimàirt

31 — Hogmanay Oidhche Challainn — Wednesday Diciadain

1 — New Year's Day Là na Bliadhn' Ùire — Thursday Diardaoin

Friday Dihaoine

Bank Holiday (Scotland)
Là-fèill Banca

2

Saturday Disathairne

3

Sunday Didòmhnaich

4

· Outer Isles from Skye ·

January
2014 / 2015

28		Sunday Didòmhnaich
29		Monday Diluain
30		Tuesday Dimàirt
31	Hogmanay Oidhche Challainn	Wednesday Diciadain
1	Bank Holiday Là-fèill Banca	Thursday Diardaoin
2	Bank Holiday (Scotland) Là-fèill Banca	Friday Dihaoine
3		Saturday Disathairne
4		Sunday Didòmhnaich
5		Monday Diluain
6		Tuesday Dimàirt
7		Wednesday Diciadain
8		Thursday Diardaoin
9		Friday Dihaoine
10		Saturday Disathairne
11		Sunday Didòmhnaich
12		Monday Diluain
13		Tuesday Dimàirt

14	Wednesday Diciadain
15	Thursday Diardaoin
16	Friday Dihaoine
17	Saturday Disathairne
18	Sunday Didòmhnaich
19	Monday Diluain
20	Tuesday Dimàirt
21	Wednesday Diciadain
22	Thursday Diardaoin
23	Friday Dihaoine
24	Saturday Disathairne
25	Sunday Didòmhnaich
26	Monday Diluain
27	Tuesday Dimàirt
28	Wednesday Diciadain
29	Thursday Diardaoin
30	Friday Dihaoine
31	Saturday Disathairne

— Notes —

Notes

Notes

Notes

— Notes —

Lynne S.
Claire
Hazel M

Asos

Scotsale

Chai

SW 57 11 12½ 7
JC 55 11 6 6½

Caledonian MacBrayne Contact Details:
Caledonian MacBrayne Ltd
The Ferry Terminal
Gourock
PA19 1QP

Tel: 0800 066 5000

www.calmac.co.uk

Hebridean Celtic Festival, Isle of Lewis
www.hebceltfest.com

Royal National Mod
www.acgmod.org

Fèisean nan Gàidheal
www.feisean.org

Shipping Forecast BBC Radio 4 – 92.4–94.6 FM,
1515m (198kHz): 00:48, 05:20, 12:01, 17:54